Why Ph

MW01504535

Learning to read is a fun and exciting time in a child's life, and being able to decode words is an important skill that gives young readers the confidence and the ability to read new and unfamiliar words. Phonics is a method of teaching beginning readers to decode by learning the spoken sounds associated with written letters and letter pairs. To become skilled readers, children must internalize these associations in order to read words without having to sound them out letter by letter or part by part. In addition, phonics instruction gives new readers the tools necessary for making the important connection between sounds and their spellings. Becoming fluent or automatic with these skills helps develop reading fluency and builds a strong foundation in reading comprehension, an important skill for academic success.

Upon your child's completion of each activity, use the provided incentive chart and stickers to track progress and celebrate your child's success.

SKILLS

- Consonant sounds
- Short vowel sounds
- Long vowel sounds
- Y as a vowel
- Letter pair blends with l, r, s

- Letter pair digraphs (ch, sh, th)
- Vowel pair dipthongs (ou, ow, oi, oy)
- Sounds of oo (as in moon and book)
- R-controlled vowels

HOW YOU CAN HELP SUPPORT LEARNING

- Work with your child in a calm, quiet setting.
- Read with or to your child every day.
- Point to a word in your child's story book and ask him or her to tell you the sounds of the word's letters. Then blend the individual sounds into the complete word.
- Go on a "letter-sound hunt" when running errands. Point out words on advertisements and buildings and have your child tell you the sounds of each letter in the words.

Consonant Sounds

Circle the consonants with the same beginning sound as each picture.

1 Bb   Dd

2 Gg   Cc

3 Dd   Cc

4 Kk   Ff

5 Ll   Gg

6 Hh   Dd

7 Jj   Cc

8 Gg   Kk

9 Ll   Ff

10 Mm   Bb

Consonant Sounds Match

Draw lines to match the consonants to the objects with the same beginning sound.

  Nn

  Pp

  Qq

  Rr

  Ss

 Tt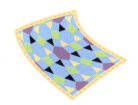

Tangled Consonants

Use a different color and trace each path to connect the consonants to the objects with the same beginning sound.

Mixed Consonant Sounds

Write the letter for the beginning sound of each picture.

1.

_____

2.

_____

3.

_____

4.

_____

5.

_____

6.

_____

7.

_____

8.

_____

9.

_____

Matching Consonants

Write the consonant that makes the beginning sound for each picture.
Then draw a line to connect the letter to another matching picture.

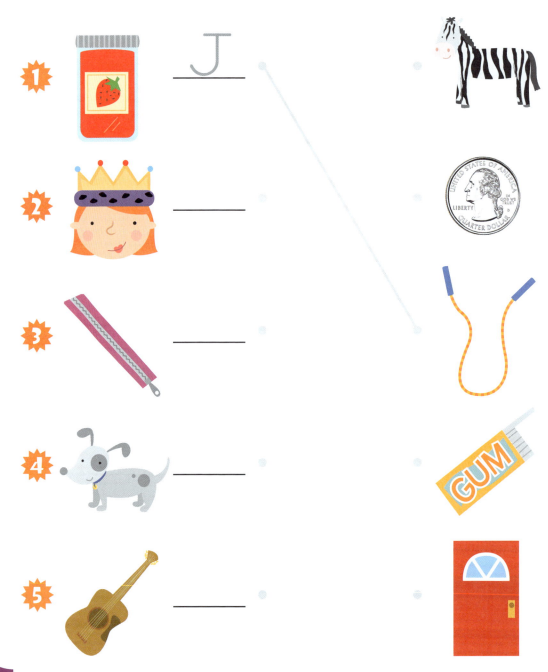

1. J ____

2. ____

3. ____

4. ____

5. ____

The Sound of Short a

Circle the pictures that have the sound of **short a** as in **cat**.

Picture Match: Short a

Draw lines to match the **short a** words to their pictures.

1 can 　　　　　　　　

2 fan 　　　　　　　　

3 cab 　　　　　　　　

4 hat 　　　　　　　　

5 hand 　　　　　　　　

6 rat 　　　　　　　　

© 2012 CTP - 7229

Hidden Picture: Short a

Color the spaces with **short a** words **brown**. Color the other spaces **green**.

The Sound of Short e

Circle the pictures that have the sound of **short e** as in **bed**.

Short e Eggs

Use a **red** crayon to color eggs with pictures of **short e** words.
Color all other eggs **blue**.

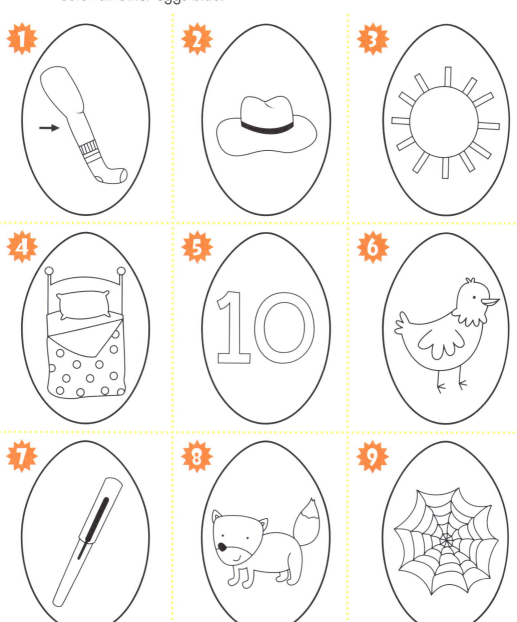

Short e Maze

Draw a line along the path of **short e** words to help the hen find her pen.

hen   bed   men

sun   pig   ten

fox

bib   leg   egg

hat   vet

fix   web   pen

Short i Pigs

Use a **pink** crayon to circle the pictures of **short i** words on each pig.

Picture Match: Short i

Draw lines to match the **short i** words to their pictures.

1 fin

2 pig

3 pin

4 fish

5 six

6 hill

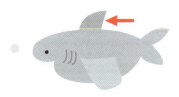

Hidden Picture: Short i

Color the spaces with **short i** words orange. Color the other spaces **blue**.

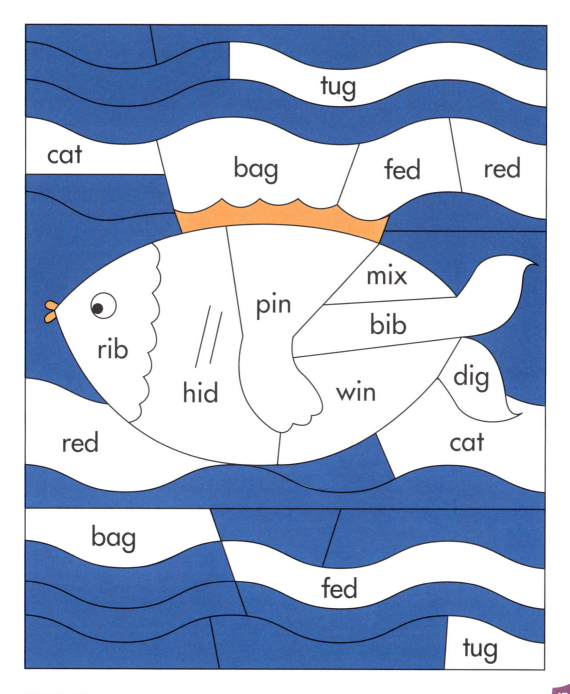

tug

cat

bag

fed

red

mix

pin

bib

rib

dig

hid

win

cat

red

bag

fed

tug

The Sound of Short o

Circle the pictures that have the sound of **short o** as in **fox**.

Picture Match: Short o

Draw lines to match the **short o** words to their pictures.

1 log

2 mop

3 box

4 doll

5 fox

6 dog

Word Scramble: Short o

Unscramble the letters to spell each **short o** word.

1

g l o

_____

2

x b o

_____

3

o c t

_____

4

p t o

_____

5

g d o

_____

6

p o m

_____

7
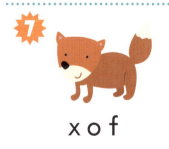

x o f

_____

8

l o d l

_____

9

k s c o

_____

Short u Umbrellas

Use a **purple** crayon to color umbrellas with pictures of **short u** words. Color all other umbrellas **blue**.

Picture Match: Short u

Draw lines to match the **short u** words to their pictures.

1 sun

2 rug

3 cup

4 bug

5 gum

6 bun

Short u Maze

Draw a line along the path of **short u** words to help the bug find his rug.

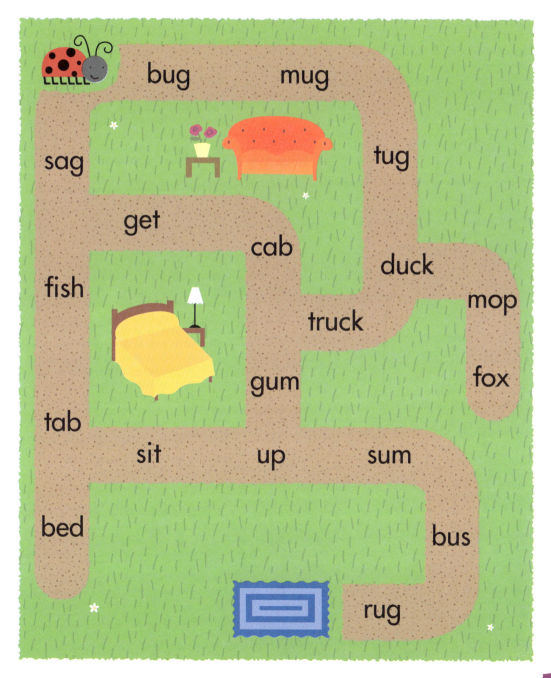

bug   mug

sag   tug

get   cab   duck

fish   mop

truck   fox

gum

tab

sit   up   sum

bed   bus

rug

Short Vowel Balloons

Use the code to color the balloons.

short a–**green**   short e–**red**   short i–**yellow**

short o–**blue**   short u–**purple**

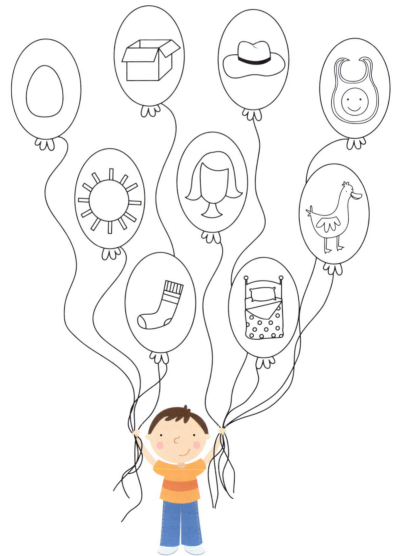

Scrambled Short Vowels

Unscramble each word and write the letters on the lines. Then draw a line to match the word to its picture.

1 sbu ___ ___ ___

2 nip ___ ___ ___

3 dbe ___ ___ ___

4 tco ___ ___ ___

5 tne ___ ___ ___

6 pli ___ ___ ___

7 hta ___ ___ ___

8 xbo ___ ___ ___

Missing Short Vowels

Look at the picture. Then write the missing short vowel.

 1

b___s

 2

h___n

 3

f___n

 4

f___sh

 5

s___ck

 6

m___n

 7

f___x

 8

g___m

 9

l___g

10

w___g

Change the Short Vowel

Change the short vowel in each word to make a new word to match the picture.

 1 cup      c a p

 2 log      __ __ __

 3 crib      __ __ __ __

 4 nut   __ __ __

 5 fin      __ __ __

 6 cab      __ __ __

The Sound of Long a

Circle the pictures that have the sound of **long a** as in **cake**.

Picture Match: Long a

Draw lines to match the **long a** words to their pictures.

1 cake

2 lake

3 gate

4 tape

5 cane

6 grapes

Long a Words

Say the name of each picture. Then circle the matching word.

1 can   cane

2 gate   gat

3 tape   tap

4 plat   plate

5 skate   skat

6 vas   vase

7 wav   wave

8 rake   rak

9 cag   cage

Picture Match: Long e

Draw lines to match the **long e** words to their pictures.

1 bee

2 sheep

3 queen

4 feet

5 geese

6 teeth

7 three

8 jeep

Long e Maze

Draw a line along the path of **long e** words to help the bee find his feast.

bee   steam   sweet

Ben

step   meal

stem

Mel   fest   steep   clean

bead

bed   sweat   feast

HONEY

Long i Kites

Color the kites with **long i** pictures green. Color the other kites red.

Long i Words

Say the name of each picture. Find the matching **long i** word in the Word Box and write it on the lines.

Word Box

smile	kite	fire
bike	ice	dime

1. _____ _____ _____ _____

2. _____ _____ _____ _____ _____

3. _____ _____ _____ _____

4. _____ _____ _____ _____

5. _____ _____ _____

6. _____ _____ _____ _____

Long o Bones

Draw lines to match the **long o** pictures to the words on the bones.

1   cone

2  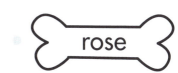 rose

3   soap

4   rope

5  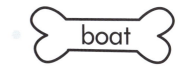 boat

Scrambled Long o

Unscramble each word and write the letters on the lines.
Then draw a line to match each word to its picture.

1 paos ___ ___ ___ ___

2 seno ___ ___ ___ ___

3 nebo ___ ___ ___ ___

4 sero ___ ___ ___ ___

5 oerp ___ ___ ___ ___

6 atob ___ ___ ___ ___

7 ceno ___ ___ ___ ___

8 rebo ___ ___ ___ ___

The Sound of Long u

Circle the pictures that have the sound of **long u** as in **cube**.

Hidden Picture: Long U

Color the spaces with **long u** words and their matching pictures **black**. Color the other spaces red.

Long Vowel Review

Write the words from the Word Box in the correct groups.

Word Box

cane	feet	cube	time	fire
cone	rose	lake	seed	music

long a

1 _____

2 _____

long e

1 _____

2 _____

long i

1 _____

2 _____

long o

1 _____

2 _____

long u

1 _____

2 _____

Mixed Vowel Review

Use a **red** crayon to circle short vowel words. Use a **blue** crayon to circle long vowel words.

tape

sun

bike

rug

cube

pig

bee

rope

bat

Y as a Vowel

Write the words from the Word Box in the correct group.

Word Box

| sky | money | try | happy |
| fly | silly | my | baby |

long e sound

1. _____
2. _____
3. _____
4. _____

long i sound

1. _____
2. _____
3. _____
4. _____

Blends with l

Write the correct beginning blend.

Word Box

| bl | cl | fl | gl | pl | sl |

1 _____ _____

2 _____ _____

3 _____ _____

4 _____ _____

5 _____ _____

6 _____ _____

7 _____ _____

8 _____ _____

9 _____ _____

10 _____ _____

Blends with r

Write the correct beginning blend.

| br | cr | dr | fr | gr | pr | tr |

1 ___ ___

2 ___ ___

3 ___ ___

4 ___ ___

5 ___ ___

6 ___ ___

7 ___ ___

8 ___ ___

9 ___ ___

10 ___ ___

Blends with s

Circle the correct beginning blend.

1

sp   sm   sk

2

sc   sp   sn

3

sc   st   sn

4

st   sm   sn

5

st   sp   sk

6

sn   sc   sm

7

sk   sn   sp

8

sm   sk   sn

9

sn   sm   sk

All Aboard the Blends Train!

Use the code to color the cars on the blends train.

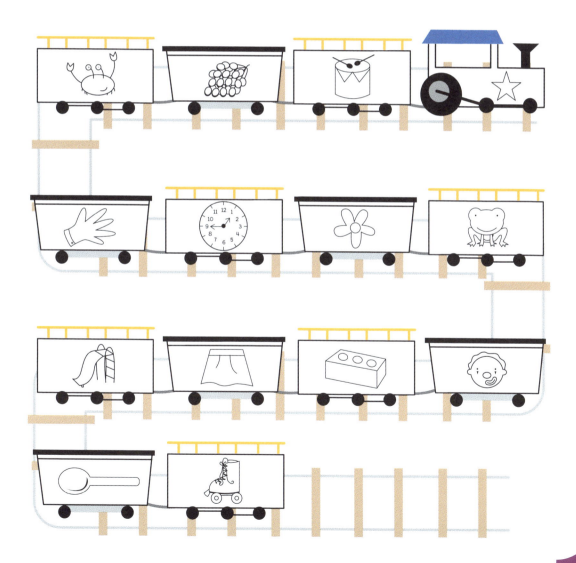

Letter Pairs-ch

Help Charlie find the treasure chest. Draw a line to make a path along the pictures that begin or end with the **ch** sound.

Letter Pairs-sh

Use a **blue** crayon to circle pictures of words that begin or end with the **sh** sound.

Letter Pairs-th

Say the name of each picture. Circle **B** if the **th** sound comes at the **beginning** of the word. Circle **E** if the sound comes at the **end** of the word.

1

B   E

2

B   E

3

B   E

4

B   E

5

B   E

6

B   E

Mixed Letter Pairs–ch, sh, th

Say the name of each picture. Then circle the letters that spell each word and write them on the lines.

 1

sh	o	ch
ch	ur	th

___ ___ ___ ___ ___ ___

 2

r	a	sh
b	e	th

___ ___ ___ ___ ___

 3

f	e	ch
r	i	sh

___ ___ ___ ___

 4

ch	o	p
sh	i	d

___ ___ ___ ___

 5

ch	i	p
sh	e	st

___ ___ ___ ___

 6

f	ee	th
t	i	ch

___ ___ ___ ___

Double o (oo)

Say each picture name. Use a **blue** crayon to circle the pictures that make the same **oo** sound as in **moon**. Use a **green** crayon to circle the pictures that make the same **oo** sound as in **book**.

1

2

3

4

5

6

7

8

9

Vowel Pairs–ou, ow, oi, oy

Circle the picture in each row that has the same vowel sound as in the first picture.

1 cloud

2  boy

3 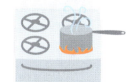 boil

4  flower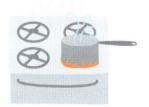

R-Controlled Vowels

Circle the picture in each row that has the same vowel sound as in the first picture.

bird

corn

fork

nurse

star

More R-Controlled Vowels

Circle the missing pair of letters. Then write them on the lines to spell the word.

1

er   ar

___ ___ m

2

ar   or

c ___ ___ n

3

or   ir

f ___ ___ k

4

ir   er

b ___ ___ d

5

er   ur

n ___ ___ se

6

ar   er

c ___ ___

7

ir   er

f ___ ___ n

8

er   ir

g ___ ___ l

9

er   ur

ch ___ ___ ch

Answer Key

PAGE 2

PAGE 3

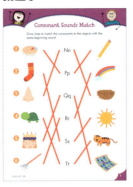

PAGE 4

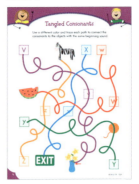

PAGE 5

PAGE 6

PAGE 7

PAGE 8

PAGE 9

PAGE 10

PAGE 11

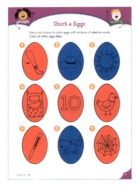

PAGE 12

PAGE 13

52

PAGE 14
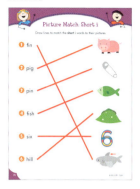

PAGE 15
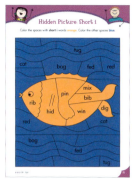

PAGE 16

PAGE 17

PAGE 18

PAGE 19

PAGE 20

PAGE 21

PAGE 22

PAGE 23

PAGE 24

PAGE 25

PAGE 26

PAGE 27

PAGE 28

PAGE 29

PAGE 30

PAGE 31

PAGE 32

PAGE 33

PAGE 34

PAGE 35

PAGE 36

PAGE 37

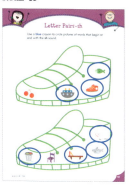

PAGE 50

PAGE 51